'What happened to him?' asked Saint Columba.

'A water monster killed him,' was the reply.

Columba touched the man and brought him back to life. Then the monster itself appeared, 'with a great roar and open mouth'. Columba made the sign of the Cross and ordered it back. And 'at the voice of the saint the monster was terrified and fled.'

Loch Ness is 35 kilometres long and very deep. Its water is full of peat from the mountains around. This makes it very dark. Even with lights, divers can't see more than a few metres ahead. The water is always very cold, but it never freezes. And it is full of fish. In fact, Loch Ness is a perfect place for a large creature to make its home.

Many people believe there is a creature there—or a family of creatures. Certainly strange things are seen. Reports as far apart as 1872 and 1932 describe the same things, in almost the same words:

'Something like an upturned boat, which went at great speed, wriggling and churning up the water'; 'a large hump-like object moving at speed'; 'something like a large upturned boat that rose from the depths.' But until 1933, when the new Glasgow to Inverness road was opened, nobody outside the area paid much attention to the strange goings-on.

Part of the new road runs along the Loch. A lot of rock had to be blasted away and a lot of forest had to be cleared. For the first time there was a clear view of the Loch from the land, and a good road along it. One spring afternoon in 1933 Mr and Mrs Mackay were driving along this road when Mrs Mackay suddenly said,

'John—what's that—out in the Loch?' Her husband stopped the car and looked. They saw 'an enormous animal rolling and plunging'.

In September of that year five people in a tea-shop overlooking Loch Ness saw something strange about half a mile out—'a snake-like head and neck which was moving up and down and turning from side to side . . . two low humps sitting in the water, and a tail which splashed on the surface'.

When they told the tea-shop owner, she took it quite calmly. 'I've seen it several times,' she said.

The newspapers heard of it, and sent reporters down. The *Daily Express* had a headline, 'The Loch Ness Monster Hunted In Its Watery Lair'. They suggested it was a 'prehistoric monster, released from the earth by the great blasting operations for the new road.' Bertram Mills' Circus offered £20,000 reward for the Monster, alive. People went on Monster-hunting expeditions and Monster-watching boat trips. Souvenir shops did a roaring trade in Monster models and tea-cosies.

BERTRAM
MILLS
OFFER A
£20.000 Rew
to anyone
who can captu
LOCH NESS MON
ALIVE
MONSTER
REWARD
FOR
MONSTER

The *Daily Mail* sent a famous big game hunter to track the Monster down. He was very excited to find huge footprints by the Loch. He did not notice that all the prints came from the same foot. Experts did, and they also found that the footprints came from a hippopotamus. They matched exactly a hippo's foot umbrella stand in a house near the Loch. The big game hunter went back to Africa.

The scientists said 'I told you so!' and for a time the newspapers kept quiet about the Monster. Scientists are always very good at explaining things away. 'Tree roots or a rotting branch,' they said to people who claimed to have seen the Monster. 'A family of otters—or a large seal . . . and are you sure you hadn't been drinking?'

This seems a little unfair. Most of the people who saw the Monster were local people, who surely knew a tree branch, or an otter, or a seal when they saw one. People began to worry in case the world thought their district was full of heavy drinkers, 'seeing things' as they staggered home. But the sightings went on—and by people so serious and respectable that they surely would not try to fool the public. Priests, lawyers, policemen, teachers, even a visiting Belgian count—they all saw it. Someone has worked out that there are over 4,000 people alive today who believe they have seen the Monster. How many more have seen it and kept quiet because they were afraid of being laughed at?

All the descriptions are alike. This is very unusual. People usually differ widely in the way they see and remember things. But everyone describes a big, humped creature, dark in colour, seven to ten metres long, with a long, snake-like head and neck.

There are very few photographs of the Monster, and there are no good ones. At

first this seems surprising. You would think that, from thousands of sightings, there would be some good pictures. But when you remember that people were trying, probably with hands shaking with excitement, to photograph something hundreds of metres out in the Loch, perhaps it is not so surprising after all. And there are one or two very interesting pictures. One, taken in 1934 by a doctor, shows what looks like a long, thin neck sticking out of the water. If it is not a large animal, it is hard to say what it might be. And movie films of the 'Monster' moving through the water look quite different from film of the wake of a boat.

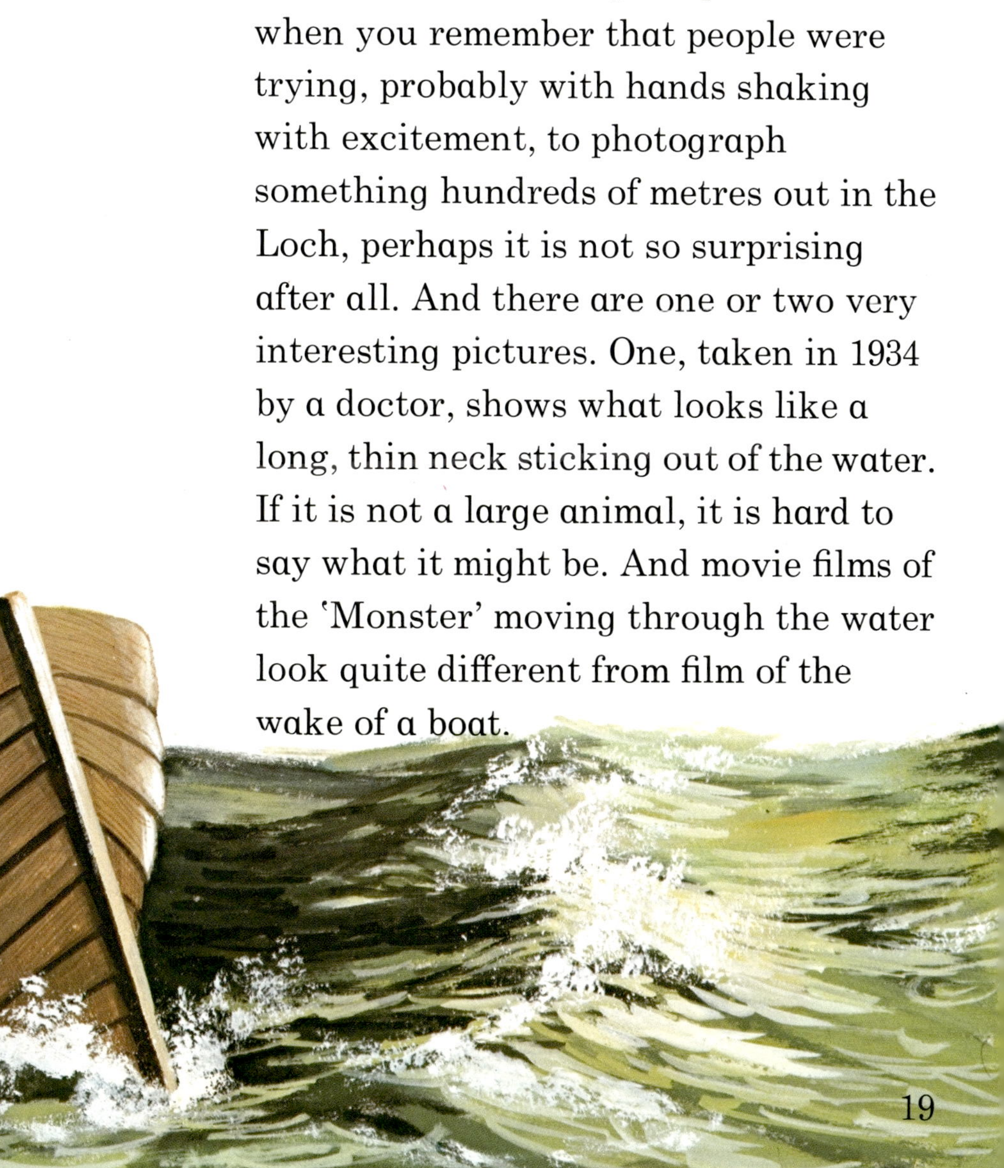

The Monster has several times frightened people in boats. It nearly overturned Alex Campbell's motor boat, and during the War a Navy motor launch hit it.

'There was the most terrific jolt. Everybody was knocked back. And there it was. There was a very large animal form, which disappeared in a flurry of water. It was definitely a living creature.'

That is what the launch's captain said. He sent a signal to the Admiralty, 'Slight damage as a result of collision with Loch Ness Monster.' The Admiralty did not believe him, and he got into trouble for not looking where he was going.

But people also believe they have seen the Monster on land. All describe it in roughly the same way—a seven metre creature humping its way along like a caterpillar, or on seal-like flippers, with a long neck that turned from side to side. Two little girls saw it on a shingle beach. They were put to bed with a big dose of castor oil. Then a farmer and his son saw it crossing the road; a driver saw it as he rounded a bend one night, and a girl on a bicycle saw it on the beach below the road. A

young veterinary student saw it and even found 'skid marks' made by its flippers. An expert agreed with him, and added, 'There was a large crushed down area in the bracken as if some over-sized cow had lain there, though no farm beast could have reached that spot.' No one believed the student. In the end he grew tired of the teasing and stopped talking about the whole thing.

Modern equipment has helped in recent 'monster-hunting.' A group of naturalists set up an Investigation Bureau in the 1960s. For months they kept watch with cameras, listening equipment and sonar equipment (for bouncing sound waves off large objects). They had several sightings and heard some 'animal-like' tapping noises, but still no pictures or film that could prove 'Nessie' was there. The RAF's experts looked at their film and said it showed something alive, and not just a boat or a shoal of fish. Then Birmingham University's engineering department tried out some new sonar equipment. Two huge, very strange objects entered the sonar beam. One moved in and out of the beam for ten minutes, dived and swam off. Another, their report says, behaved in a truly amazing fashion by animal standards.

The hunt went on, with cameras, sonar and even a midget submarine. Some strange hangers-on joined the hunt. One claimed the Monster was really a spaceship from Venus. In 1971 a whisky company offered a million pounds to anyone who delivered 'Nessie'

to them. Meanwhile the sightings went on, mixed with hoaxes which made people doubtful about the serious sightings. A Mr O'Connor took a 'Monster photo' of what turned out to be three large, air-filled polythene bags. . .

In August 1972, a team of experts picked up an echo and, with an underwater camera, they photographed what looked like a huge flipper. The actual echo-traces and photographs would not mean much to you or me. But to experts they showed a large, moving object, though no creature they recognised, except one. Could it be a plesiosaur? You will not find one in the zoo, though there are plesiosaur bones in museums. Descriptions of 'Nessie' add up to something very like the plesiosaur. But it is a prehistoric creature. It died out 70 million years ago.

Well, so did a fish called the coelacanth. At least that is what scientists believed until Professor JLB Smith caught a coelacanth, alive and wriggling!

All this time we have talked about a Monster. But the Loch is quite big enough and deep enough for a family of large creatures. Have these animals been living there all these years? Is there even, perhaps, a link between them and old tales of dragons and sea-serpents?

We should not laugh until something has been proved. Professor Smith wrote, when he caught that coelacanth, 'Why is this discovery so important? It is a stern warning to scientists not to be too fixed in their opinions.'

Not all scientists are dogmatic about 'Nessie'. Some are getting very excited indeed. If the creatures in the Loch are not plesiosaurs, are they some other prehistoric creature? Or a giant newt? Or even a completely unknown species? 'At the very least,' says an American professor, 'it will be a very great discovery.'

Macdonald's colourful and exciting series of paperbacks now include the following titles:

Macdonald Mysteries:
The Mary Celeste
The Abominable Snowman
Lost World of Atlantis
The Loch Ness Monster
Anastasia
The Masked Prisoner

Macdonald Ghosts:
The Ghostly Army
Haunting at Hampton Court
Ghosts of Culloden
Macbeth the Murderer King
Caesar's Ghost
Who Betrayed Guy Fawkes?